MW01097234

WHAT THIS KID WANTS ADULTS TO KNOW ABOUT GRIEF

WHAT THIS KID WANTS ADULTS TO KNOW ABOUT GRIEF

BRYCE A. FIELDS
as told to Bradley Vinson

PUBLISHING
2020

Copyright © 2019 Bryce A. Fields
All rights reserved.

Printed in the United States of America

Published by VC Publishing • PO Box 536, Argyle, TX 76226

Visit the author's website at www.ThisKidsGrief.com

All rights reserved. No part of this publication may be reproduced, stored in a retrieval system, or transmitted in any form or by any means without the prior written permission of the publisher. The only exception is brief quotations in printed reviews.

For quantity orders, contact publisher directly at info@vinsoncs.com

Editing by: Carol Thompson
Cover Design: Bradley Vinson
Cover Illustration: Lionel Milton • www.lionelmilton.com

Although the author and publisher have made every effort to ensure that the information in this book was correct at press time, the author and publisher do not assume and hereby disclaim any liability to any party for any loss, damage, or disruption caused by errors or omissions, whether such errors or omissions result from negligence, accident, or any other cause.

First Edition

Publisher's Cataloging-in-Publication Data

Names: Fields, Bryce A., author. | Vinson, Bradley, author.
Title: What this kid wants adults to know about grief / Bryce A. Fields as told to Bradley Vinson.
Description: Argyle, TX: VC Publishing, 2020.
Identifiers: LCCN: 2019920315 | ISBN: 978-0-9894976-0-2
Subjects: LCSH Grief in children. | Bereavement in children. | Loss (Psychology) in children. | Children and death. | Children--Counseling of. | BISAC FAMILY & RELATIONSHIPS / Death, Grief, Bereavement | FAMILY & RELATIONSHIPS / Parenting / General | SELF-HELP / Death, Grief, Bereavement | RELIGION / Christian Living / Family & Relationships Classification: LCC BF723.G75 F54 2020 | DDC 155.9/37--dc23

DEDICATION

For my family and especially my Mom

TABLE OF CONTENTS

VIII

ACKNOWLEDGMENTS

Our family, Camp Agape, counselors, teachers and our church. We want you to know you are appreciated.

We thank you for all you have done to help Bryce on his grief journey. You hold a special place in his heart and he wanted to make sure you all are acknowledged for the work and care you have shown him and other little hurting hearts.

What you have done for him and others, in part, is what has fueled his desire to help other children (and adults) in their grief and give them tools for their journey.

Thank you, thank you, thank you!
Bryce & PawPaw

INTRODUCTION

The insights and experiences found within this book are unique to Bryce, which he has given over the past few years since his little sister (my granddaughter) Alanna, passed away. He desires to help adults better understand the hurting children in their lives better.

The children you care for will surely have their own unique experiences based on their particular loss and other factors. Remember, every child is unique and needs care specific to their individual needs.

We also believe there are some universal truths to healing on the journey of grief. The unique views found within these pages can be used to help you help the little hurting hearts in your life travel this hardest of journeys in a way that leads to healing and wholeness.

Along the way, you will find Bryce's insights spawned dialogue from me in call-out boxes like the one below.

> Share this book with your children, use it as a conversation starter, or let it help you explore and discuss grief in a safe space.

In some cases, my insights are to help translate what he was saying!

We pray you will use this book to help you see into the little hurting hearts you care for and build (or strengthen) a bridge to communication and understanding them better.

Bradley Vinson (PawPaw)

"WHEN MARY THOUGHT
JESUS HAD DIED, SHE WAS GRIEVING TOO,
BUT JESUS WENT ON TO A BETTER PLACE,
JUST LIKE OUR LOVED ONES"

- Bryce

1

FOR ADULTS

PARENTS, CAREGIVERS, EDUCATORS, AND ADVOCATES

Before my grief, I always felt awesome. Life was the best. When I was little, I thought everything was lollipops and unicorns.

Then that morning, after the accident, I was in shock. I didn't know what to do. I cried because everybody else was crying. It lasted for days, I cried, and cried, and cried.

I feel most sad when it's time to go to sleep because I'm not thinking of much stuff. In the quiet times when there's not much to do except think, and I'm not thinking of anything, it's easy to start thinking of things that make me sad. My grief comes mostly at night.

My life is really different now [since Alanna passed away] mostly because I don't get to do things with her anymore. I think about her a lot, and she's in my memories. I still do some of the things we used to like to do together—sometimes alone, sometimes with my little brother—like building a fort.

Parents, lay off a little bit, let the kids speak. Don't ask them a bunch of stuff. Sometimes we just don't feel like talking about it (or thinking about it) and asking a lot makes it come back up.

We need space to work through some of our healing stuff on our own, **but be available to us when we want to talk.**

> Here's a great way to be ready when they are.
>
> Use the H.E.L.P. method:
>
> H - have the hard, honest conversations about grief and loss.
>
> E - express yourself, show a healthy example of grieving.
>
> L - lean in and love more, be more affectionate, give a lot more hugs and caring touch.
>
> P - patience, be willing to 'circle back' and experience their changing grief as they age.

I was six when my sister passed away, and I cried a lot more then because everything reminded me of her and it made me feel bad. As I'm getting older, I don't cry as much because I have more tools to help me, but things will still trigger my grief.

We (kids) can keep our emotions inside for a long time (and not show them), sometimes to keep you (grownups) from feeling bad.

I think it was great that you [PawPaw] talked to my teachers before school started, so they knew what happened. It's the best way for teachers to understand how to help us when we are sad.

I didn't cry or anything during school, but if I did, it was good that the teacher knew why I was crying.

> A great resource that helps with the process of preparing others for your child's grief is the 'Grief Inventory Sheet.' You can get a copy from www.ThisKidsGrief.com

When parents don't help the teacher understand, the teacher won't know what to do. They may send the child to the principal's office or something. The parents should let the teacher know—not the student.

Adults should ask their kids if they'd like to go to therapy. It can be a good thing. It worked for me, and I'd like to talk to my therapist again because it was cool to talk and play with him.

It's okay to come to talk to me when you're [parent/caregiver] sad about something because if you feel sad, I want to know. I don't like making you feel sad, though, so sometimes I will not tell you how I feel.

> Remember, they are children, not your counselors. Sometimes we need to shelter them from our grief—not hide it entirely, but it shouldn't be the predominant thing they see from us.

We need you to take us to another grownup (counselor) we can trust and talk to that can keep a secret.

When my babysitter asked me what happened, I didn't like that. When regular people I don't know well ask me about Alanna, it makes me feel weird, but it's okay for therapists and counselors to ask. If you could help me know what to say to these people, it would make me feel better. I don't want to answer their questions, so maybe you can tell me how to say that to them.

I'll have a wave of emotions—I'm happy, I'm sad, I'm happy. I'm learning to understand these emotions.

Sometimes I get scared to tell my grownups how I feel because I don't want to make them sad; I don't want them to cry. **That would make me feel bad.**

> We have to make it safe for kids to share—or not share—their feelings.

We feel like sometimes, if we tell you about our grief, it will make you feel bad, and we don't want that.

> Adults have to be willing to release "total" control of helping our children with their grief and be okay with not knowing some of the things going on with them in their grief. Being able to release the need to know everything for the sake of your child's healing is worth it. Remember, just like there are things you don't burden your children with, they feel the same way about us.

Parents, be okay with telling your kid it's okay for them to talk to other [trusted] people about their grief. You have to be okay not being the only person your kid talks to feel better.

> Just being okay with it is not enough. You have to TELL them that; they have to hear it and understand you're okay with it.

Watching horror movies makes me think about things. They make me think about a series of events that could happen. I worry about things. Like when I watch "Jaws"— a shark attacking people makes me think of other things, and things falling on people. Everything could lead to something that could be bad, like an electric pole could break and electrocute people.

This is also called "catastrophizing," always thinking something bad is going to happen. I believe this feeling comes directly from the loss of his sister. When their simple ride to school became a tragic car accident that took the life of his little sister, it's easy to see how he can imagine bad things lurking around every corner.

I don't think like that a lot now, but I do get scared that something can happen to other people I care about, like my PawPaw. The only thing I fear more than anything else is PawPaw falling down the stairs.

Well, that and clowns. I don't like clowns; they're creepy. They try to make you laugh, but it's not funny.

And spiders. I'm really afraid of spiders.

I slipped on the staircase in our home once—or four times (it sounds a lot worse than it was), but it really affected him. He would have dreams about me falling, getting hit by cars, all the worst stuff in a "Final Destination" movie...it's a new burden he lives with that I cannot fix or change for him. He's always waiting for the next shoe to drop and that something terrible will happen to me.

This may be one of the greatest burdens for an adult with a grieving child. Not being able to tell them the simple things that can put most other children at ease, such as, "I promise, I won't let anything happen to you," "I'll be fine, no need to worry about me," or "nothing's going to happen to me." Those phrases are no longer in the toolbox of care for an adult with a grieving child.

HOLIDAYS AND SPECIAL OCCASIONS

Holidays and other special occasions are different now because I don't have Alanna, and I don't get to do things with her anymore like I used to.

Sometimes I feel like I'm missing out on things that I never got to do with her. I'm missing out on the opportunity to do things with her and share experiences with her.

I only remember the big moments in life. As time passes, I forget a lot of things especially because I'm taking in a lot of stuff into my brain—a lot of stuff is going on.

Christmas is a big one because I don't have the opportunity to play with her and see her toys and stuff.

It bothers me for people to know and remember the day Alanna died, but [instead] I would love for people to know about her birthday. Her birthday is still here, and I want people to remember the special day of when she was born [and], how old she would be now.

Remembering when she died is a sad day. I want people to remember a happy day [like] the day she was born and celebrate her life.

I feel nervous during big family gatherings because I don't want to start crying and ruin the day for everyone, so I act shy.

I get more nervous as more people come around, but them coming is okay. It's good to have people around, but my feelings can go up and down.

I may feel bad because it's the holidays, but I want to know it's okay for me to feel bad and that I [1] should not feel like I'm going to ruin a special moment when everyone is happy, and [2] feel embarrassed if I cry or something and make everybody else feel sad, and, [3, I'm] ruining the entire Thanksgiving or Christmas or special day.

> It's important that we TELL our grieving child that their tears
> or emotions will not ruin our day. Express that we love them,
> we know that the day can be hard for them, and that we
> understand how they might feel or act. Giving them the assurance
> that their tears or shyness will not affect us in a negative way
> helps give them confidence to be themselves. Let the day happen
> as naturally as possible.

I always anticipate the holidays being good.

I just want to keep it cool and think about good memories. I
don't start feeling sad just because the holidays are coming
because I WANT them to be good. It's just [that] sometimes
I think about things that make me sad because Alanna is
not around.

> It's cool that children can come to that level of understanding. I
> believe sometimes we adults feel that children can be emotional
> just for the sake of being emotional; however their feelings can
> change based on what's going on (just like they do with us).
> It's only natural that a child's emotions can fluctuate.

The holidays are not sadder than other days; they're really
not. I'm busy making new happy memories, but while I'm
making new memories the old memories will come up too.
Old memories are hard to forget—both good and bad ones.

Some good old memories can feel bad because they can't be repeated (like playing with my sister). **New good memories are good, but they are not better than old good memories.**

I enjoy having family around [for] playing games and more. Having them around helps me feel good.

Family photos during the holidays make me feel sad because I can look back at the photos later and see what's different—where we are, the people in them and stuff. When I look back at the photos, I can see that Alanna is not in them.

I look at old pictures and see how happy Alanna was in them. We'll take pictures again this year, and she doesn't get a chance to be happy in the photo because she's gone. That's probably when I feel the worst—when we're recording things, I can go back and look at later.

> Adults need to know that even though the moments can be happy, as time goes on and more photos are made, the child will have a catalog of happy memories and reminders of who is missing from those happy memories.

GOING TO THE CEMETERY

I understand when we go to the gravesite on Alanna's birthday or a special occasion (like when someone's visiting or something). But when it's a random day, like, "Hey, let's go on Saturday" I get upset about going because I may have had something I wanted to do.

It's different if family is visiting and they say they want to go. But [on] other random days if I had the option to stay home, I would—but [at this age] I can't.

The idea of going all the time makes it feel like it's not special anymore. [It's] like if you go every Saturday, it's not special; it's just going repeatedly. If you go every year on their birthday, [then] that's special.

Sometimes, I might want to go because I'm sad and going might make me feel better, but that doesn't happen a lot.

If either the kid or adult can explain why they don't want to go (or can't go because of work or something) and we all talk it out; it makes it better.

THINGS ADULTS THINK THEY KNOW, BUT THEY REALLY DON'T

Sometimes adults think they have all the answers, and know all the things we need to help us feel better, but they don't. Some things just don't have answers.

You cannot fix everything, and you have to be okay with that. This thing cannot be fixed because you cannot bring my loved one back.

Sometimes just because I'm laughing or having fun doesn't mean I'm not sad.

Sometimes I want to be alone and don't want your help right then, but I probably want you to comfort me later. Just because I'm crying doesn't mean I need you right then.

Sometimes I don't want help, I just want to be alone to think.

I might cry in front of you. That usually means I want help. But if you find me crying in my room away from you, I probably want space and time to work through it on my own.

Asking is a good idea instead of just coming to me and trying to comfort me.

My grief changes as I get older. Some of the things that worked when I was younger may not work when I'm older.

> We have to be willing to "circle back" and re-experience their grief with them as they age. A 10-year-old's grief is different from when they were six years old, and things we think they may be past (as far as healing) can return as they develop mentally and socially.

NOTES/IDEAS

2

FOR KIDS

What makes us so different from other kids is that we realize it's not always good. They might think, "Oh, the world is awesome, everything in it is awesome; nothing's bad." That's what I thought. But when grief hit, I felt this full mass of stuff get put on my shoulders— like Alanna passing away, and I didn't get to say anything to her before she passed away.

I would tell other grieving kids who have lost a loved one to **seek help as soon as possible—immediately**. Go to a parent or trusted adult or self soothe.

Crying helps me get over being sad (I know most people think you cry only when you're sad). Crying is like medicine; it helps me release and get the sadness out.

Sometimes I'm by myself when I get sad and have to figure out a way to work through it on my own. I may cry and think, "What should I be trying to do to help myself feel better about my grief?"

I seek help from an adult in my life, mostly my PawPaw. He helps me a lot, too. He tells me, "It's okay," and [he] comforts me.

I really don't tell everybody [every friend], but I tell my closest friends [that I've lost a loved one]. I don't really bring it up to them, but if they ask me what's going on with me (if they see that I'm sad or not talking very much) I'll tell them because we are really close; but if other people ask, I won't.

Once I tell them [friends] about Alanna, they're okay with it. They don't treat me different or anything.

Other kids might ask a bunch of questions about it (what happened and stuff like that), but my close friends don't.

Have confidence to talk to your adult about how you feel. You can pray to God for strength.

Get your feelings out!

I think my grief is just like [similar to] a kid who lost a parent. We've all lost a family member. If you lost a close friend, that might be different because you may not have that special connection like family members do.
You can have a special connection, but it's not like a family connection.

6 TOOLS KIDS CAN USE TO HELP ON THEIR GRIEF JOURNEY

These tools help me express my grief instead of trying to hold it all in, get angry or stressed about my feelings.

1. Prayer
When you feel sad you can pray to God about your grief and it will help you through the night (when I usually pray), and through the days to come. Nothing would happen if God didn't help.

2. Reading
When you read, it's like the pages are talking to you. It's like you're in the book because you can see all the characters and feel what they feel.

3. Writing

Writing is a good way to get all your emotions out on paper, and you can go back and read them later. It's okay for my parents or counselors, [and other adults] to read them. It's like I'm telling them about my feelings without having to talk about it.

When I write [journal], I also add the date so I can go back and read it later and see how I was feeling that day and how things are different now. All that helps.

4. Art

You can draw your emotions out on paper, and just like writing you can look back at it later. You can draw things about angels or anything that can help you get out how you're feeling.

You can draw your favorite animals, places or anything to help you remember your loved one and help you to get better.

5. Talking to people with similar grief experience

We are able to share and help each other. If the person doesn't have grief, talking to them helps them prepare for when they do have grief. They can come back to you for advice.

6. Remembering someone you love that passed away

Have pictures of your loved ones and holding them (it makes you feel like you're holding their hands). You pray while you're doing this and ask for strength to make it to tomorrow.

SOME OF MY FAVORITE THINGS:

• Alanna's picture (sometimes I rub it, sometimes I grab it and squeeze it)

• Her crazy animal toy that makes funny sounds

You don't have to do all the things. You can just do the ones you think will help.

NOTES/IDEAS

3

WHAT ADULTS (AND SOME KIDS) WANT TO KNOW

Sometimes, I feel mad at my loved one for dying. Is that bad or wrong?

No, it's your emotions. You're letting out how you feel. It's not a bad thing, you're upset that your loved one is not here. It's nobody's fault.

> Anger is a natural reaction. It is one of many emotions that come from grief just like sadness, fear, and more is natural. We just have to make sure we grieve in a healthy way.

What do you want grownups to know about your grief?

My grief is sometimes a big wave, which is like a lot of emotions; and sometimes it's like a small wave. But either way, it's an emotion. I want you to understand that I can have good days and bad days.

Sometimes I can go for long periods of time without thinking about my loved one (who passed away). Does that mean I don't love them anymore?

No! It's good to not think of the time they passed away, but to focus on good things. The memories are always there of your loved ones, even if you don't think of them all the time. For me, it's usually a few days before I think of my loved one. The amount of time between you thinking about them doesn't mean you don't love them. When I'm playing with friends or reading or doing homework, I'm not thinking about Alanna, but the memories are always there.

When I'm missing my loved one really bad, what are some things I can do with those feelings?

You can ask someone for help by saying, "I'm going through this really tough time, can you help me?" You can write in your journal or draw pictures. You can look at videos or photos of your loved one. These things can help you let it out and cry if you need to.

Is it okay to cry if I'm sad? Some people tell me I'm supposed to be grown up and not cry, what do you think of that?

That's not right! It's okay to cry. Sometimes adults cry too. Everybody cries. The person who feels this way about you crying should stop feeling that way. Crying is like medicine, it helps you feel better.

Sometimes, I see my parent or grandparent crying. Are they okay?

Yes! They're just sad about their loved one that passed away. They're expressing their love. This could be a good time for you to be able to comfort them, you can hug them and tell them it will be "okay."

How can I help my parents, grandparents, or other adults with their sadness?

Comfort them in a way that only you can comfort them. Just like my PawPaw comforts me in a way no one else can; everybody has their special way to do that.

Sometimes teachers are afraid to talk to their students about the loss or their grief, but they really care and want to let their students know they are there for them if they need it. What is the best way a teacher can support a grieving child?

The best thing to do is comfort them. The teacher needs to ask how the child is doing. Don't make them feel weird if they look sad or cry in class.

How would I help my friend whose parent just died?

You have a special connection with friends so you can comfort them in your special way. Let them know it's okay, and sometimes people go through things that are hard. Let them know you care about them.

What do you wish other kids would ask you?

How I am doing. How do I feel. I always ask kids how they are feeling if they look sad or something, but they never ask me how I'm feeling.

Have questions of your own, we'd love to hear them. Drop us an email at info@vinsoncs.com and we'll respond as soon as we can.

NOTES/IDEAS

4

FAITH AND FAMILY

That morning in the car, I didn't say anything to her, I was just chilling. I think about now what I could have said.

Everything just piled up—what am I going to do? How is this going to work?—questions like that.

When Alanna first passed away, I didn't know what happened. I was confused. I just saw everyone else was crying. I didn't know it was something bad, I just went along with it. Then after a few days, I had a dream, and God told me what happened.

He [God] told me, "Alanna's passed away, and you're not going to see her again until you go to Heaven with Me." After that, I just got sad, really sad.

I remember talking about it [Alanna's passing] with
[you] PawPaw, but God told me again and helped me to
understand. When you told me, I kept forgetting because I
would dream about Alanna reappearing. She was just lost.
She didn't pass away. She was somewhere in the world.
She kept popping up every time I had a dream.

It was weird because every time I'd dream, she'd keep
popping up, and as soon as I was getting ready to hug her,
she'd disappear. It would make me mad in my dream.
Wherever I was at in my dream, she'd be there.

Then God came to my dream and said, "She's gone," then
after that I stopped dreaming like that.

Before, I remember asking Mommy, "Who made God?" I
remember asking her, "who made 'something?'" "God" "Who
does this?" "God," then I'd ask her, "Who made God?" She'd
say, "Nobody made Him," but I wasn't sure about that.

I was like, "Where did God come from?" [One time when
Alanna and I were having "Church" at home] Alanna
prayed, and then I knew God was real. I wasn't sure before,
but then as soon as that moment hit [when Alanna prayed],
I knew for sure God was real.

I didn't ask her again. But then another question popped up when all the things happened. "What is happening?"was the question. It was related to "What does God do?" and those two questions just fell on my shoulders— really heavy, questions like "Why did you do this?" "Did God make this happen?" I was really sad.

Alanna helped other people before I did, and her passing away fueled my desire to help people, and PawPaw [you] nourished it and kept it going.

Posing after church on May 8, 2016.

Three peas in a pod. August 2015 at Great grandparents' home near Jefferson, TX.

Alanna,
always smiling.

After church on
Easter Sunday in
2016 with our cousin,
Kelvin "Bubba".

I am my brother's keeper! Camp Agapé Family retreat 2018.

Big sister shenanigans, April 2016.

We all geaux for LSU! At BeBe's and PawPaw's house.

Lazy Summer nights, nothing better than lovin' on PawPaw.

First Christmas at BeBe and PawPaw's new house, December 2015. BeBe lets us decorate the fireplace and Minnie Mouse gets center stage.

Alanna's beauty shines as she prepares backstage at her last pageant, March 2016.

5

WHAT THIS KID TAUGHT ME

As I was helping Bryce with this book, I realized more and more how important it would be to add to the discussion and speak directly to parents of grieving children. I do this to encourage you, to give some insight into the talks and experiences Bryce and I had in the making of the book and to give you things I discovered about myself and our shared grief journey.

Here is a short list of things that jumped out at me after contemplating and absorbing all that was happening around us and to us:

The words I say about grief mean a lot.
As we went through the videos, transcription and interviews I did with Bryce to create this book, I noticed when I used certain words he'd push back on my use of them. I would say

"Alanna died" or "Alanna's gone," he would push back on that in his own gentle way, but push back none-the-less. He doesn't like the words "died" or "death." He prefers "passed away," "she's with God," or "transitioned." Some may see these as semantics, but I believe there's a deeper reason. True, he knows she's gone from this earth, but he sees her as living in his heart, not dead.

What hammered that home for me is from a meeting we had with his teacher when he was about to attend a brand new school (we met with the educators to advocate for him and gave the teachers the knowledge and resources to work with him as a grieving child).

During the meeting the teacher asked, "How many children do you all have at home?" and before my wife or I could answer, Bryce said, "There's three. PawPaw can explain that to you." We were all a bit startled by that, but then I explained to the teacher that we have the two boys (Bryce and his little brother) and one angel girl who's in Heaven.

Bryce clearly feels that Alanna is with us. It's not fantasizing or imagination because we speak of her and are open with how we feel about her. She's always "around."

Bryce doesn't see death as the end, but instead a transition to the next stage of life with God.
He feels that others who may not be Believers say "dead" or "death" are saying that it's over, that's the end. He doesn't see it that way.

We cannot teach our children peace. They have to witness and experience it (they have to find it for themselves). Deep grief and great joy can coexist.
As adults this is a hard one. I feel if I shelter them,
it brings peace, and at a smaller level, it does. Children have
to have their own peace without our intervention.

Death doesn't separate.
Bryce's connection with his sister is not broken. It is
physically broken, but they are connected. Unless you're an
only child, the people that are with you most of your life are
likely your siblings; not your parents or your spouse.
It's your siblings. Bryce and Alanna were two years apart,
and at the age of six the person who's supposed to be with
him for a greater part of his life than any other person,
passed away.

I grieve the fact that the person that is meant to be with
him the longest is gone, but I learned from him that
through his connection with her, she will always be with
him because he carries her with him.

I have to accept I'm not the only source of his healing.
I have to trust him in his desire to trust others in
helping him heal. This doesn't minimize his need for me
to participate in his healing process, but I have to be
comfortable with others playing key roles in his journey
without my input.

NOTES/IDEAS

ABOUT THE AUTHOR

Ten-year-old Bryce relishes his role as "big brother." At the age of six, that role was redefined with the loss of his little sister. His tender servant heart has led him to serve other grieving children including his little brother, TJ, with insight and wisdom he has gained from his unique journey.

He is an aspiring engineer, speaker, musician, and Minecraft YouTube sensation!

FOR MY PAWPAW...

"A LOT OF THE WEIGHT OF SADNESS LIFTED
WHEN I WENT TO CAMP AGAPE.

TALKING TO YOU AND MAKING THIS BOOK
LIFTED A LOT OF STUFF OFF MY SHOULDERS."

- Bryce

HOW TO CONTACT BRYCE & HIS PAWPAW

If you're interested in an innovative approach to connect and care for grieving kids, we can help. For more information about keynotes, trainings, workshops, interviews and coaching by Bryce and his PawPaw (Bradley Vinson), visit **ThisKidsGrief.com** or **BradleyVinson.com** for details.

If you would like to order additional copies of this book, they can be purchased at **ThisKidsGrief.com** and many other well-known book retailers.

To purchase bulk copies of this book at a discount for your organization, please contact us at **info@vinsoncs.com**.

Visit **ThisKidsGrief.com/resources** for an ever-growing list of resources, including books, videos and activities to help on your healing journey.

THE END

We hope you found this book helpful!

This book also comes in an eBook and audio version for your mobile devices.

Share this much-needed resource!
Ask your library, school, counselor's office
& other places that care for little hurting hearts to order this book so others can be helped by it too.

THANK YOU!

Made in the USA
Middletown, DE
14 January 2020

83180119R00038